a nap...

or just your attention.

A dog will happily go on any adventure...

© Kent Dannen

or spend all day doing nothing with you.

He'll help with the chores...

and carry any load you ask.

He loves to give kisses...

and will console you when you cry.

He supports your hobbies...

and takes your interests seriously.

He'll jump through any hoop for you!

A dog
doesn't care
if you go
shopping
all day...

and watch sentimental movies all night.

He'll sleep late with you on the weekends...

© Chris Harvey/ardea.com

or get up early and exercise with you.

He'll be your escort to wherever you want to go...

© Bonnie Nance

and he'll NEVER leave you for a younger dog!

OK, so a MAN will never be as good as a **DOG**...

But that doesn't mean you shouldn't love him or marry him. Just make sure your MAN gives you...

all of the RESPECT...

friendship...

and unconditional LOVE that a dog would
(and that you deserve)!

He's content with just a squeak ball...

and doesn't get upset if he's defeated.

He loves to play...

© Cris Kelly

and he looks cute in the morning.

He doesn't snore so loudly that it wakes you up...

and his face is always smooth.

He shows emotion with facial expressions...

© Sharon Eide/Elizabeth Flynn

and greets you with a smile when you return.

A dog walks you to the door when you leave...

And he looks adorable eating meat off a bone!

and more ice cream than you will...

He'll always eat more cookies...

knowing he'll play with them
and protect them.

You can trust a dog with children...

© Chris Harvey/ardea.com

and your parents will approve of him!

Family is the most important thing in his life...

and is PATIENT when you're busy.

© Bonnie Nance

has cute bad breath...

never steals the blankets...

© Lynn M. Stone

eats leftovers without complaining...

He also likes ALL of your friends...

and will pick up the mail for you.

scratches his own back...

has no clothes to wash...

At least a dog will help with the dishes...

SURE, dogs can be a lot of work...

They need to be fed, bathed, brushed, coddled, babied, taken to the doctor when they're sick, encouraged, supported, cleaned up after, and made to feel they are the absolute MOST important being in your life...

But, HOW is that different than a man?

and he only
wears the
outfits
that you
approve!

© Tara Darling

and isn't afraid to cry...

he readily forgives...

He melts your heart with his puppy eyes...

or how much you weigh!

and he doesn't care one iota
about how you look...

devoted...

he's affectionate (even in public)...

Hugs on demand are the norm...

and pants, but doesn't want sex.

knows how
to beg and
when to
beg...

LOVES to cuddle...

has cute feet (not stinky ones)...

He barks at others (not at you)...

AND, has plenty of HAIR!

doesn't understand the word "ego"...

honest...

authentic...

He is LOYAL...

and LOVES taking long walks.

LISTENS...

makes you laugh...

gives
without
wanting
recognition
or reward...

A dog also lives in a constant state of delight...

and NEVER misses the toilet!

wouldn't think of complaining
about the food...

doesn't tell you how to drive...

For starters,

a dog comes home when he's called...

SURE, men are great...

Once in a while, when somebody's MOTHER did a good job, you'll find a MAN who is kind, intelligent, funny, attractive, polite, AND loyal. HOWEVER, at other times, a woman is better off just hanging out with her DOG, who is all of these things and MORE. There are countless reasons WHY A DOG IS A BETTER MATCH THAN A MAN. Here are just a few...

For Katia Bugger,
the inspiration for this book

Published by Willow Creek Press
P.O. Box 147, Minocqua, Wisconsin 54548

Editor: Andrea Donner
Design: Donnie Rubo

Library of Congress Cataloging-in-Publication Data

Heath, Vivian, 1957-.
  Dump him, marry the dog! : why a dog is a better match than a man /
Vivian Heath.
     p. cm.
  ISBN 1-59543-369-4 (hardcover : alk. paper)
  1. Dogs--Pictorial works. 2. Dogs--Humor. I. Title.
  SF430.H37 2006
  636.70022'2--dc22

                              2006000929

Printed in Canada

Dump him,
Marry the DOG!

Why A Dog is a Better Match Than A Man

by VIVIAN HEATH

WILLOW CREEK PRESS

Dump him,
Marry the DOG!